Unique Intricate Mandala Coloring Book For Adults Relaxation

50 Amazing Mandalas Coloring Book Featuring Original Hand Drawn Designs For Stress Relief, Meditation, Calmness & Happiness (Vol. 3)

By
Thrive Coloring Books

HAVE A QUESTION OR CUSTOM REQUEST? LET US KNOW.

EMAIL:info@thrivecoloringbooks.com

WEBSITE: ThriveColoringBooks.com

This Coloring Book Belongs To:

____

____

____

MORE BOOKS FROM THRIVE COLORING BOOKS

VISIT THE LINK BELOW FOR MORE BOOKS FROM THRIVE COLORING

http://bit.ly/thrive-coloring

HOW DO YOU LIKE THE BOOK SO FAR?

COPY & PASTE THE LINK BELOW TO LEAVE/WRITE A FEEDBACK ON AMAZON

IF UNDECIDED YET, KEEP ON COLORING AND LEAVE THE REVIEW LATER

HAPPY COLORING

DID YOU ENJOYED COLORING THIS MANDALA BOOK

If YES, THEN SHARE THE LOVE WITH YOUR FRIENDS AND FAMILIES OR GIFT THEM ONE AND LET THEM ALSO CONTINUE THE FUN

IF YOU ENJOYED COLORING THIS BOOK, TAKE A PICTURE OF YOUR LOVELY COLORING PAGE AND SHARE IT TO THE WORLD ON AMAZON.

FOLLOW THE LINK BELOW TO WRITE A FEEDBACK ON AMAZON

GET IN TOUCH WITH US

JOIN THE THRIVE COLORING BOOKS ONLINE COMMUNITY

EMAIL:info@thrivecoloringbooks.com

Website: www.thrivecoloringbooks.com

FACEBOK PAGE: @thrivecoloringbooks

Thank You